IT IS WRITTEN

BY: Stacy DuBose-Hindsfeet

Table of Content

Dedication

I dedicate this book to all men and women. This book is to encourage every soul and testify of the goodness of the Lord. The Lord has a purpose and plan for every living soul. His written word is our destines waiting to be fulfilled through us. "If ye be willing and obedient, ye shall eat the good of the land:" (Isaiah 1:19).

Acknowledgement

I acknowledge my Lord savior Jesus Christ. He has inspired me to stay yielded to his will and be obedient to his beckon and call. I acknowledge my daughter Eboni and to everyone that has been instrumental to my process of success.

Foreword

The word of God is truly our biblical instructions before leaving earth. Prophetess Hindsfeet has been one who testifies of the goodness of God daily. Leading many to the feet of Jesus. I've known Prophetess Hindsfeet for about five years and she's truly a beacon of light. This book is in the timing of the Lord truly. We're in a time and age where people want to give up on God and his word. This book "It Is Written" will be an inspiration to all. It's a testimony of Gods goodness to all humanity. The word of God tells us they overcame by the blood of the Lamb, and by the word of their testimony (Revelation 12:11).

With many different parables of others' lives in the bible; helps us to reflect in our lives today. All scriptures are given by inspiration of God(2 Timothy 3:16). We can always refer to the word of God for instruction that will lead us to a prosperous outcome that is profitable for our own lives. As a child of the Highest I've had many obstacles that has led me to understanding why the word of the Lord is my guide. It teaches me and nurtures me. My life is truly rooted in the word of God. I admonish everyone to place their lives in the hand of the Lord.

Sincerely, Prophetess Iyana Boose

Introduction

Greetings to all I'm Servant Stacy Dubose-Hindfeet. Hindsfeet is the name that God has given me on this strategic journey . A call of obeisance and faith. "It is God that girdeth me with strength, and maketh my way perfect. 33 He maketh my feet like hinds' feet, and setteth me upon my high places" (Psalm 18:32-33 KJV). " It Is Written" book is about all my miraculous provision made by the Lord. It holds some of my greatest testimonies and victories in Christ Jesus. On this walk with God, he has always made a way for me and kept me. The Lord spoke to me thirty years ago aby his spirit and said when you're led, you're fed. My life has been one of sacrifice and a love affair in Christ. I've never had a love like this before. I pray this book ministers to everyone the love of the Lord; and persuades all to take him at his word. "And my God will meet all your needs according to the riches of his glory in Christ Jesus" (Philippians 4:20). If you love me, you will keep my commandments. What God orders he pays for; and I ask God every day to order my steps in his word.

Chapter 1

The Drawing

At an early age I became interested in fashion. This is one of my gifts. I worked at Saks fifth Ave, Marshall fields, and Charles A. Stevens. I dressed people and coordinated their clothes for corporate America from head to toe. There were six of us and I was the youngest wardrobe consultant. I was chosen to go to the meetings to represent the staff; I met with the president and vice president of the store, with the concerns of the employees. I was never afraid to speak up and I have always fought for the people. Now that I am saved, I know it was only God. From there I managed a boutique up North. I had a driver who picked me up from Hyde Park and take me to the North side every day. I managed the boutique for three years and owned it for three years. In the world we would say we're lucky. However, on the hallelujah side you're either blessed or cursed. With mismanagement I was evicted from my store and apartment in the year of 1989. The next year I found out I was pregnant in my tubes, I was shocked. I hadn't taken any birth control in 15 years, I almost died. During the surgery I had a vision of Jesus on the cross and I said if he could go through this I could take and endure what I was going through. God was drawing me, but no one told me these things. The next year God saved me in 1991 and filled me with the Holy Ghost at my friend house. Glory be to God I had a radical salvation. See, I was the life of the party and got people ready for the party. I picked out what they would wear I taught all my friends how to step; I was a stepper since I was 14 years old. I was on the dance floor and the Lord spoke to me that he needed me; and I said me? From that day on I began ministry in Hyde park 30 years ago in Harper's Court. Salvation is truly a process you must die to be born again surrendering your will to Christ. Daily repenting from your sins; after repentance comes forgiveness. 3 Jesus answered and said unto him, Verily, verily, I say unto thee, Except a man be born again, he cannot see the kingdom of God (John 3:3). Things I used to do I don't do anymore. God has blessed me to be sold out for thirty years, Glory be to God!

Chapter 2

I'm Saved

Repent ye: for the kingdom of Heaven is at hand (Matt 3:2). The Lord has used my voice as one crying in the wilderness. Every day I tell the Lord have your way in me I'll go where you want me to go, I'm committed to you I'll say what you want me to say. 7 But the Lord said unto me, Say not, I am a child: for thou shalt go to all that I shall send thee, and whatsoever I command thee thou shalt speak.8 Be not afraid of their faces: for I am with thee to deliver thee, saith the Lord. 9 Then the Lord put forth his hand and touched my mouth. And the Lord said unto me, Behold, I have put my words in thy mouth (Jeremiah 1:7-9) . Being just a babe, I didn't understand what I was doing but I obeyed and said yes Lord and I'm still saying yes. Yes, every day; I've been praising God with great persecution, great pain, and great rejection I've learned that rejection is for our protection. I've sown in tears and I'm reaping in joy. Rejoice, and be exceedingly glad: for great is your reward in heaven: for so they persecuted the prophets which were before you (Matthew 5:12). The greatest miracle is salvation I thank God for saving me. I thought everybody would be happy for me, but it was the opposite. I was hated for his name sake. 35 For I am come to set a man at variance against his father, and the daughter against her mother, and the daughter in law against her mother-in-law. 36 And a man's foes shall be they of his own household. (Matthew 10:36). Psalm 27:10 says,

"When my father and my mother forsake me, then the Lord will take me up". This isn't everyone's testimony, but it's truly mines. So, I love God for being my Father , Mother, Sister, and best friend. God's love has sustained me I die daily so Christ can live in me. I have been crucified with Christ; it is no longer I who live, but Christ who lives in me; and the life which I now live in the flesh I live by faith in the Son of God, who loved me and gave Himself for me (Galatians 2:20). The word disciple comes from discipline we must deny ourselves and pick up your cross. Jesus called his twelve disciples to him and gave them authority to drive out impure spirits and to heal every disease and sickness (Matthew 10:1) . "I am sending you out like sheep among wolves". Therefore, be as shrewd as snakes and as innocent as doves (Matthew 10:16). Praise God it was the beginning of my journey and walk with God. God saved my soul and made me whole. I forsake all for the sake of the gospel. Even my own child thirty years later God is still manifesting his word to me. There was song that said, "when I gave it up that's when he blessed me, that was my testimony against all odds I made a choice now I rejoice". In the beginning I was broken and weeping so hard when I heard that song. Years later it makes me so happy that God has kept me, strengthen, and healed me by his grace. God empowers us to live and walk a life full of the Holy Ghost. Faith, perseverance, joy, love, longsuffering, patience, meekness, temperance. The fruit of the spirit is what God continues to perfect in all of our lives. These are the characteristics of Christ. On this journey a lot of people want the blessings; but don't want to go through the process of salvation. We are to work out our own salvation with fear and trembling (Philippians 2:12). God have to deliver us from all unrighteousness, for without Holiness no man shall see God. The scriptures God gave to me was (Psalm 51: 1-2) thirty years ago, and I'm still saying it, 1Have mercy upon me, O God, according to thy lovingkindness: according unto the multitude of thy tender mercies blot out my transgressions.2 Wash me thoroughly from mine iniquity and cleanse me from my sin. (Psalm 51:7)Purge me with hyssop, and I shall be clean: wash me, and I shall be whiter than snow. God will keep you if you want to be kept. He has kept me from falling for his glory. Now unto him that is able to keep you from falling, and to present you faultless before the presence of his glory with exceeding joy (Jude24:1). God can keep you if you want to be kept!

Chapter 3

The Call

The very beginning of my walk God sent me out, it was on

hands training. As I stated, it started at Harper's court in the

year 1991 the Lord has given a public ministry. Hyde park

has always been a community that embraced all

nationalities. People could come and enjoy themselves,

winning and dining day and night. Today, thirty years later it

is called downtown Hyde park. God led me to people whom I

didn't know, and the holy spirit spoke through me. One lady

wanted to commit suicide God had me go to the lady not

knowing what I was going to say and afraid. God said to me

be not afraid , it is not you that speak I have put

the words in your mouth. I saw the lady's demeanor change right before my eyes, hallelujah Jesus. People would be playing chess and God would send me to certain ones. The words weren't always welcomed I was cursed and hated for it, just like the bible states. However, I continued to obey God no matter what. He told me that it was my call to obey and believe him. Thirty years later I'm telling the world can't nobody do you like Jesus. God even sent me to businesses in Hyde Park to tell them they were closing; no one believed me and yet not one word God has spoken through me has fallen to the ground. God's word shall not return void, It has come to pass. As I was out ministering strangers would approach me and ask if I was hungry. If I said yes, they fed me, blessed me with whatever I needed it was supplied. And how shall they preach, except they be sent? as it is written, How beautiful are the feet of them that preach the gospel of peace and bring glad tidings of good things! (Romans 10:15). 12 And when you go into a house, greet it. If the house is worthy, let your peace come upon it.13 But if it is not worthy, let your peace return to you (Matthew 10:12-13).God had given me a ministry going into houses. Not knowing where I was going; God has always performed his word for his glory. It is God that doeth the work; people think it's them. All he is looking for is a yielded and available vessel. Does not the potter have power over the clay, from the same lump to make one vessel for honor and another for dishonor? (Romans 9:21). All glory, honor and praise belong to God. Ask yourself this question "Is God getting the glory out of my life"? This is a walk of great humility totally depending on God.

Chapter 4

I Got Power

This whole journey I boast on the power of the Holy Ghost.

It's not by power nor by might but by my spirit says the Lord.

I'm telling you people we can't do anything of ourselves.

(Philippians 4:13) declares, I can do all thing through Christ

that strengthens me. Jehovah is Lord that does the work; he

is just looking for a yielded vessel. On this journey you will

see miracles for God's glory. I was sent to Grand Rapid's

where my cousin was diagnosed with cancer; it was the year

1996. She was hospitalized in Cleveland Ohio and all my

family came to visit and pray. She needed a miracle! God had me to stay in her room and pray in the spirit for three days and three-nights Jesus raised her up. She stayed for ten months at the Hope Lodge. Where I spoke the word of God repeatedly to her. She confessed the healing word with her mouth, you must confess the word with your mouth. I was there to lift up the name of Jesus in the midst; that he may draw all men unto him. There was a lot of Jews there and God favored me. I was asked to pray every night. They would come get me from my room; it was the Jesus in me. I prayed for healing in the name of Jesus; and God did the impossible. I was bold as a lion, telling the people about the goodness of Jesus. Everyone received it. I was sent home with my cousin to continue to feed her naturally and spiritually by God's grace. He raised her up and delivered her and today she is telling people about the goodness of Jesus. She was also featured on a cancer calendar. The Lord is a healer of all our diseases. We must believe the report of the Lord and speak what his word says. Who forgiveth all thine iniquities, who heals all thy diseases;(Psalm 103:3). I've been sent to hospitals where the signs on the door said do not enter, the security that was sitting outside the doors asked, " Are you going in there"? I responded by the spirit of the living God he is sending me in there. When I prayed demons were cast out a garbage can was used for deliverance. The person was resurrected by the power of God. Glory be to God! She is alive and well today. Praise God what is impossible with man is possible with God. Signs, wonders, and miracles follow those that believe. Every day and in every way, God want to use you for his Glory.

Chapter 5

Grace To Run This Race

What an exciting life to be used by God! God sends me to different regions in different seasons. When God says his grace is sufficient that's what he means (2 Corinthians 12:9). Grace is empowerment; I didn't know what that meant in the beginning of my salvation. I didn't know when you are chosen by God it's for the purpose of a holy calling (2 Timothy 1:9). Now we have received not the spirit of the world but the spirit which is of God. That we may know the things that are freely to us of God. Which things also we speak ; not in the word which man's wisdom teaches but which the holy Ghost teaches comparing spiritual things with spiritual. But the natural man recieveth not the things of the spirit of God for they are foolishness unto him; neither can he know them because they are spiritually discerned (1 Corinthians2:14). 10 According to the grace of God, which is given unto me, as a wise master builder, I have laid the foundation, and another buildeth thereon. But let every man take heed how he buildeth thereupon. 11For other foundation can no man lay than that is laid, which is Jesus Christ (1 Corinthians 3:10-11).

Chapter 6

Watch Your Posture

The word posture means an attitude of the mind, a feeling, point of view or mood. God thoughts are not like our thoughts and his ways are not like our ways. So, we want God perspective and not our own. Our opinions mean nothing; it's God's will that's best for us. We must have the mind of Christ; Let this mind be in you that was in Christ Jesus(Philippians 2:5). (Jeremiah 32:18-19;NIV) 19Great are your purposes and mighty are your deeds. Your eyes are open to the ways of all mankind; you reward each person according to their conduct and as their deeds deserve. On this journey it's yes, all day and in every way. Our attitude affects our altitude. I want to go higher in the Lord and praise him all the days of my life. I love God with all of my heart; God rewards us by the cleanliness of our hand (Psalm 18:24). The Lord has rewarded me according to my righteousness in him. As for God, His way is perfect; the word of the LORD is flawless. He is a shield to all who take refuge in Him (Psalm 18:30). We must submit and commit our ways to the Lord. A life of dedication to God is what we were created for. Boasting on the Lord is what I do; If you don't want to hear about the goodness of the Lord and his faithfulness, you don't want to see me. The Lord is rewarding me. My cousin bought me a CD by Tri City years ago called "testify"; it's truly my testimony for the glory of

God. That's what this work is all about. The word of the Lord

says to do all things without murmuring and

complaining(Philippians 2:14).

Chapter 7

Pass The Test To Be Blessed

1Therefore, being justified by faith we have peace with God. 2Through him we have also obtained access by faith into this grace in which we stand, and we rejoice in hope of the glory of God. (Romans 5:1-2). If we believe the word of God that all things work together for the good of them that love the Lord and are called according to his purpose. We must embrace the good, bad and the ugly seasons of our lives. For the trying of our faith is more precious than gold. God inhabits in the praises of his people. It's easy to praise God when things are going well; but can you praise them when they're not? God gave me a crazy praise through it all, you can praise your way through. Our trials are to make us better not bitter. We must pass the test to be blessed. The Lord is building character in all our lives. The flesh must die daily, we must not faint. Although our outward man perishes, yet the inward man is renewed day by day (2 Corinthians 4:15). We have this treasure in our earthen vessels that the excellence of the power, may be of God and not of us (2 Corinthians 4:7). Always barring about in the body, the dying of the Lord Jesus. That the life also of Jesus might be made manifest in our mortal flesh (2 corintians4:10). Search me oh God and know my heart; try me and know my thoughts, see if there be any wicked way in me and teach me in the way of everlasting (Psalm 139:23). I tell God everyday let my thoughts be his thoughts. I want to walk like Jesus; give me the mind of Christ. We should always take upon the characteristics of Christ; he is our example to live by. Too much is given, much is required. If we suffer with him, we will reign with him. I, therefore, the prisoner of the Lord, beseech you that ye walk worthy of the vocation wherewith ye are called,(Ephesians 4:1). Lord, continue to take us higher heights and deeper depths. Lord, I pray you make us vessels of honor for the master's use. You get the glory every breath we take and every step we take; you get the glory. Be ye therefore followers of God as dear children and walk in love as Christ also have loved us; and have given himself for us an offering and sacrifice unto God as a sweet-smelling savior(Ephesians 5:1). Thank you, Jesus ; Let no man deceive you with vain words, for because of these things cometh the wrath of God upon the children of the disobedient, be ye not partakers with them for ye were sometime darkness but now are ye light in the Lord; walk as children of light. For the fruit the spirit is in all goodness and righteousness and truth proving what is acceptable to the Lord(Ephesians 5:9).

Preparation proceeds the blessing.

Chapter 8

He's Always On Time

It is written, Eye hath not seen, nor ear heard, neither have entered into the heart of man, the things which God hath prepared for them that love him (1 Corinthians 2:9). God has been good to me. It is written if it had not been for the Lord who was on our side, where would we be. All of us are born for a purpose. It's all about God and not about us but God's will being done on earth as it in Heaven. But now, O LORD, You are our Father; We are the clay, and You, our potter; And all we are the work of Your hand (Isaiah 64:8). God is using me to write this book. I started this project in the year

1997. It was completed in 2011; this material was given to a computer whiz that I trusted to edit the book and he ran off with it. God spoke these words to me "trust in me with all thine heart and lean not to thine own understanding" (Proverbs 3:5-6). The first thing that God told me in the beginning of my salvation was I want to deprogram your mind. I would be led by God to go to different services. Every time, no matter how big the crowd, I would be called out. And the word from the Lord God was dealing with my mind. I would fall out under the power of the Holy Ghost. I've let God have his way in me from the very beginning. Not even knowing what it would cost me and that is everything. What an honor to be used by God. It is written "And everyone that hath forsaken houses, or brethren, or sisters, or father, or mother, or wife, or children, or lands, for my name's sake, shall receive a hundredfold and shall inherit everlasting life" (Matthew 19:29). This is what was required of me. I didn't know anything about anything. I just told the Lord yes and he gave me the strength in my heart, mind, and body to do it. I died that he may live. We must deny ourselves every day, pick up our cross and follow him. You are a disciple of Jesus Christ, living a life of discipline. We must thank God first for salvation, which is our greatest gift from God. Money cannot buy salvation it is a gift from God, that no man can boast. God is a spirit and they that worship him must worship him in spirit and in truth (John 4:24). As we go through our tests, trials, and tribulations we can become bitter or better .It is written, we must ask God to create in me a clean heart and renew the right spirit in me (Plasm 51:10). "Restore unto me the joy of thy salvation; and uphold me with thy free spirit." (Psalm 51:12). Man looks at the outward appearance, but God looks at the heart. We must be patient and full of hope. God is in control we must trust him and his timing. Continue to praise God. God's blessing is from the inside out praise is weapon. As we deny ourselves Christ lives within. For thou are Great and does wonderous things, thou are God alone (Psalm 86:10). Holy Spirit is a gentleman, and our comforter. The Lord does not force anyone's will but if you draw nigh unto God, he will draw unto you. In love and kindness, he has drawn us. It's only the love of God that has sustained me. There is a song that states "you can search high and low it doesn't matter where you go you won't ever find nobody like the Lord". I am a witness that if you suffer with him you will reign with him. Humble yourselves in the sight of the Lord and he shall lift you up (James 4:10). Promotion comes from the Lord.

We must stay humble before the Lord. Wherefore he saith,

God resisteth the proud, but giveth grace unto the humble."

James 4:6). In our wilderness experience we are being made

meat for the master's (God) table. Our adversity is an

opportunity for God to show himself strong in our lives and

transforms us to be more like Christ. God is building

character in his people he is teaching us obedience and

perfecting of our faith through the affliction. We have to be

steadfast in the faith, unmovable I don't care what the

situation or circumstance is we must stand on the word as

we grow glory to glory and faith to faith in the Lord. We are

in the school of obedience we must remember that all things

work together for the good of them who love the Lord and

are called according to his purpose. I have to say every day that all things are working for my good, it may not feel or look good. Nevertheless, it is working for our good. Our situation ought to keep us in prayer, it is our communication with God. Man should always pray and not faint. The effectual fervent prayer of a righteous man avails much (James 5:16). We're in a time of God's set time to fulfill destiny and purpose according to his will. It's raining all over the world. The portals of Heaven are open right now. The Lord is not slack concerning his promise, as some men count slackness; but is longsuffering to us-ward, not willing that any should perish, but that all should come to repentance (2 Peter 3:9). It is written Seek ye first the kingdom of God and all of his righteousness and everything else will be added unto you (Matthew 6:33). But the God of all grace, who hath called us unto his eternal glory by Christ Jesus, after that ye have suffered a while, make you perfect, stablish, strengthen, settle you (1 Peter 5:10-12). He's doing it for me, and he'll do it for you too. God rewards our righteousness every day. He also told us whatever was fair he would pay. It is a true statement only what we do for Christ will last. The latter rain is greater than the former. The Lord tells us to learn to be content in whatever state we are in have a spirit of gratefulness of God's faithfulness. The prophecies are coming to pass; things spoken years ago because God said it. Won't he do it! He's doing exceedingly abundantly more than we can ask or think according to the power that worketh in us (Ephesians 3:20). He's manifesting it right now. The book was born on the river Sonder Luxury Suites 61 W Erie God sent me there and paid for my stay. Everything there was new. God was letting me know he is settling and establishing me right now. God launched several of my businesses in California in 2020 during the Pandemic, it's been my greatest season. I am a fashion consultant today; I dress my client from the inside out. God rewards your faithfulness, if you are faithful over a few things, he will make you ruler over many (Matthew 25:23). 45 Blessed is she that believed: for there shall be a performance of those things which were told her from the Lord (Luke 1:45).